SEPAR*ATIONS*

THE HOSPITAL

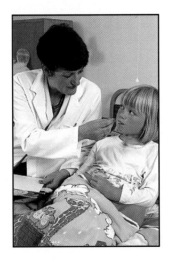

■

by Janine Amos
Illustrated by Gwen Green
Photographs by Angela Hampton

■

Gareth Stevens Publishing
A WORLD ALMANAC EDUCATION GROUP COMPANY

Please visit our web site at: www.garethstevens.com
**For a free color catalog describing Gareth Stevens Publishing's list of high-quality books
and multimedia programs, call 1-800-542-2595 or fax your request to (414) 332-3567.**

Library of Congress Cataloging-in-Publication Data

Amos, Janine.
    The hospital / text by Janine Amos; illustrations by Gwen Green; photography by
Angela Hampton.
      p. cm. — (Separations)
    Includes bibliographical references.
    Summary: Uses letters, stories, and informational text to explain what to expect when
you have to go to the hospital.
    ISBN 0-8368-3091-1 (lib. bdg.)
    1. Hospitals—Juvenile literature. 2. Hospital care—Juvenile literature. [1. Hospitals.]
2. Medical care.] I. Green, Gwen, ill. II. Hampton, Angela, ill. III. Title.
    RA963.5.A47   2002
    362.1'1—dc21   2001054953

This edition first published in 2002 by
Gareth Stevens Publishing
A World Almanac Education Group Company
330 West Olive Street, Suite 100
Milwaukee, WI 53212 USA

This U.S. edition © 2002 by Gareth Stevens, Inc. First published as *Hospital* in 1998 by
Cherrytree Press, a subsidiary of Evans Brothers Limited. © 1998 by Cherrytree (a member
of the Evans Group of Publishers), 2A Portman Mansions, Chiltern Street, London W1M 1LE,
United Kingdom. This U.S. edition published under license from Evans Brothers Limited.
Additional end matter © 2002 by Gareth Stevens, Inc.

Gareth Stevens cover design and page layout: Tammy Gruenewald
Gareth Stevens series editor: Dorothy L. Gibbs

Printed in the United States of America

1 2 3 4 5 6 7 8 9 06 05 04 03 02

Contents

Dear Steven,

I'm in the hospital waiting for my operation. My mom went to the cafeteria to get a snack, so I thought I'd write you a letter, like I promised.

When I first got here, I was a little scared. There are loads of people, and everyone's busy. It felt strange knowing that I'd have to sleep here. I thought I'd have to put my pajamas on right away and get into bed. My nurse's name is Sara. She's fun. She told me I could keep my jeans on. Then she showed me the green gowns and masks the doctors will be wearing tomorrow for my operation (just like on TV). She told me exactly what will happen to me, so I'm not as worried now.

I have to have an injection before the operation. I told Sara I really hate shots. She says they'll put some special cream on my hand to make it go numb. Then I'll only feel a tiny prick. I met the doctor, too. She poked around at my stomach and told me a Knock-Knock joke.

The main thing I'm worried about is that I won't be able to go skiing with you after Christmas. I'm afraid to ask, in case they say no.

See you,

Jake

P.S. There's another boy here named Robert. We're going to play cards and watch television together.

Dear Jake,

It sounds like the hospital's ok. If you're still there next Saturday, Mom promised to drive me over to see you. She says children's wards don't have special visiting hours, so we can stay all day. We'll bring you some chocolate cake. Yum! Your doctor sounds nice. Why don't you go ahead and ask her about skiing? It's better than worrying about it.

You'll have a new video to watch soon. Mom and I sent it to the hospital for you.

See you,

Steven

What's the Matter?

Emily was in her room. She was building a Lego space station. Emily loved to build with Legos, but, today, the pieces seemed too small and slippery. Her head ached. A fly buzzed at the window, and the sun was streaming in. Emily was hot and tired. She needed a drink.

Emily went to the kitchen. Her mom was there, talking on the telephone. Emily's mom spent hours on the phone. She could even cook at the same time! As soon as Emily came in, however, she put down the phone.

"What's the matter?" asked Emily.

"Nothing, dear," her mom said brightly.

"Something's going on," thought Emily, getting herself some juice.

The next morning Emily woke up early. On her way to the bathroom, she passed her brother Dan's bedroom. He was still sound asleep, so Emily tiptoed down the hallway. Then she heard voices from her mom's and dad's room.

"I haven't said anything yet," her mom was saying. "We'll tell her when the time is closer."

Something about her mom's voice made Emily stop and listen. Then she heard her dad say, "She won't want to go, not Emily. She'll really put up a fuss."

"They're talking about me," thought Emily. "They're going to send me away!"

Back in bed, Emily thought about her dad's words. Where did he think she wouldn't go? Why were they sending her? Her heart began to pound, and she felt a little sick. Had she done something wrong?

All morning Emily watched her mom closely. She helped her mom clean up after breakfast. Then she helped her wash the car.

When the telephone rang, Emily jumped.

"Claire's mother is on the phone," said Emily's mom. "Would you like to go over there for lunch?"

Emily shook her head. She wanted to stay home.

At lunchtime, Emily couldn't even eat. Her headache was worse, and she wanted to cry. Just waiting for something to happen was awful. She went and sat down on her bed. Then her mom came in.

"Is something the matter?" she asked.

Emily burst into tears. "You're sending me away!" she shouted.
"I heard you!"

Emily's mom sat down next to her. She gave Emily a big hug.

"I'm so sorry, Em," she said. "I didn't mean to worry you. You have to go into the hospital next week and stay there for a few days. The doctors are going to run some tests on you. But I'll be staying there, too."

"Who'll take care of Dan?" asked Emily.

"Nana's coming," said her mom. "It's all arranged."

"Will you be with me all the time?" asked Emily.

"Yes," replied her mom, "and, before then, we'll visit the hospital together. You can see the children's ward and meet some of the nurses. Would you like that?"

Emily nodded.

Finally, the day came for Emily to go into the hospital. She packed a bag to take with her. She put in two pairs of pajamas, five story books, three comic books, a toothbrush, and her old Mickey Monkey.

"I don't mind going to the hospital," said Emily as she climbed into the car. "The thing I didn't like was not knowing."

"I understand that now," said Emily's mom. "I did it wrong, didn't I?"

"That's OK," Emily said, smiling. "Let's go!"

11

Dear Auntie Jan,

Thanks for your card. Sorry about my writing. It's hard to write lying down! I feel much better since I had the operation, but I can't go home yet. I have to stay in bed. When I first got to the hospital, lots of doctors and nurses checked me. They gave me X-rays and took blood tests. I couldn't have any breakfast before the operation. Afterward, I had lots of tubes in me. I wasn't scared because the nurses told me what they were all for, and Mom slept on a cot next to me.

I thought it would be boring here, but it's ok. The nurses are great, and there are lots of other children. A teacher comes in every day with work for me. I still have to do math, even in the hospital! I have a good time, though. Yesterday I made a cake. Lying down! It seems like I'll have to be here for ages. I bet everyone at school will forget about me. Sammie will get to be Kim's best friend. They're doing a project together, working on it after school.

Please write soon.
Love, Anna

12

Dear Anna,

It was great to get your letter. You sound as if you're doing very well in the hospital. I'll be coming to see you next week.

Are you worried about what's going on at school while you're away? I remember feeling like that when I was sick and couldn't go to work. Is there anyone you can talk to about it — your teacher, a nurse, or your mom? They might have some ideas for keeping in touch with your friends at school. How about writing to Kim and the others?

I'll see you next week, Anna. If you do any more baking, save a piece of cake for me!

Love,
Auntie Jan

13

Feelings: Going to the Hospital

When you first find out that you have to go to the hospital, you might feel worried and wonder what it will be like.

■ It's natural to be concerned about a new situation. If you are feeling nervous, talk to a grown-up about it, and try to work out all your worries together.

■ Some television shows about hospitals show frightening scenes of operations with lots of blood and big, beeping machines. Children will often remember these scenes when they think about hospitals. Remember that these scenes have nothing to do with you. They're not real anyway! The hospital is simply a place that tries to help sick and injured people get better.

■ Some children may not like the thought of being away from home. They worry about sleeping in a strange bed, without all their usual things around.

■ Some children may worry about leaving their pets behind. They wonder if anyone will take care of them. And will they be taken care of properly?

Injections

Lots of people hate the idea of getting an injection. If you're really worried, tell your parent and make sure the nurses know. Ask if some anesthetic cream can be put on before the injection. This cream makes your skin numb so you won't feel the needle. And don't look at the needle! Yell if you have to, but hold your body still. Remember, the needle prick will last only for a second.

■ Children seem to worry about their friendships, too. Anna is afraid that the girls in her class will forget about her. She worries that her best friend will start to like someone else more.

■ Some children worry about what they might be missing out on at school, and they wonder if they are going to be able to catch up with everything later.

15

Getting Ready to Go

If you need to go into the hospital, here are some things you can do to prepare yourself:

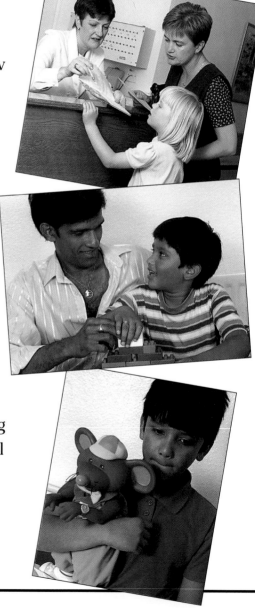

▪ Find out why you have to go to the hospital and what will happen to you there. Ask how long you will have to stay at the hospital. If you don't understand everything, keep asking. If your parents have any questions, they should ask the hospital staff. See if you can visit the hospital before you go in to stay.

▪ Share any worries you have with an adult. One of your parents can stay with you in the hospital. If your parent will need to go home at any time, figure out, together, who could come stay with you during that time.

▪ Pack a bag to take with you. You might want to pack a favorite toy, a special drinking cup (even a bedtime bottle if you think it will help), storybooks, coloring books, crayons, games, soap, a hairbrush, a toothbrush and toothpaste, cool daytime clothes (a hospital is often hot), and two pairs of pajamas.

- If you have a pet, ask someone in your family, or a friend or neighbor, to take care of it. Tell them what your pet likes and doesn't like, so you won't worry about it while you're gone.

- Ask if a friend from school can visit you in the hospital to help you keep up with what's going on there. Ask your teacher what the class will be doing while you're gone. You might be able to do some schoolwork in the hospital.

Emergency

If you're rushed to the hospital in an emergency, you won't have time to prepare, but there are things you can do to help yourself cope. Take some deep breaths to help keep yourself calm. Remember, the nurses, doctors, and paramedics are doing their jobs as fast as they can to help you. Ask someone to explain what's happening. Ask a nurse to hold your hand.

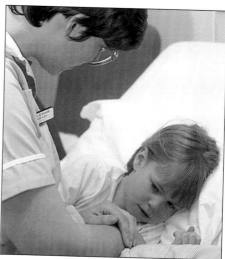

17

Dear Steven,

Thanks for the video. It's great! I watched it twice. The second time, I watched it with Robert, the boy I met here.

I had my operation, and it was ok. I knew what was going on because the doctors and nurses talked to me all the time. Mom was with me, and she asked some questions, too. They gave me an injection to make me go to sleep, so I didn't feel them doing the operation.

My stomach's a little sore, but the nurse said that will go away in a few days. Mom sleeps here at the hospital in a chair that pulls out to make a bed. Dad's coming to see me this afternoon.

I'll be home on Saturday, so Mom says you can come to our house instead of the hospital. (You can still bring the yummy cake.)

I'm keeping a hospital diary of everything that happened while I was here. I can take it to school and show the class.

See you,

Jake

Hospital Diary

Monday
In children's ward. Mom and I met Sara, the nurse. I went to the playroom and met a boy named Robert. Mom filled out a form. Sara checked my height, weight, and blood pressure. The ward is busy and noisy. Everyone is friendly. Video next to my bed — great! Won't be able to have breakfast tomorrow before my operation, so I stuffed myself just before bedtime. Food here is ok.

Tuesday
Woke up early. Sign on my bed: NIL BY MOUTH. (It means I can't eat or drink until after the operation.) They just put cream on my hand, and it is starting to go numb. So I won't feel the injection.

photo of me and Robert in the playroom

Wednesday
My stomach is sore, but Sara gives me medicine to make it feel better. Got up and went to see Robert. Don't remember much about yesterday. Worst part was leaving Mom. She couldn't come into the anesthetic room. It was kind of scary then, but everyone was talking to me, so it was OK. Woke up and Mom was here. Had breakfast, lunch, and dinner! Watched a new video from Aunt Cathy and Steven.

Thursday
Doctor says I'm fine. I can go home on Friday.

Thank you for taking care of me. My stomach is fine now. Skiing is great. I'm getting pretty good. Afterward, we have hot cocoa with whipped cream on top to warm us up. Happy New Year to you all.
Love from
   Jake Narraway

The Children's Ward
St. Michael's Hospital

19

Feelings: In the Hospital

Hospitals are big, busy, noisy places. At first, they might seem strange and a little scary. There are unusual smells, lots of new people, and large machines. Everything is different from home or school.

■ Because a hospital is new to them, and because everyone is so busy, some children feel very small and powerless. You might think you can't ask questions, but never be afraid to ask.

■ Don't ever think your worries are silly. They're not! Some childen worry that their clothes will be taken away, that a nurse they don't know very well will give them a bath, or that they will be different in some way after an operation. These concerns are very real. No matter what your fears are, talk to a nurse or a doctor about them.

■ For most children, the time they must stay in the hospital will be short. Some children, however, need to stay longer. Some quickly get used to hospital life and might even worry about leaving.

■ Some children get bored in the hospital. They find it hard to read or do schoolwork. They feel cut off from the real world and fed up with everything.

Having an Operation

If you need to have an operation, you might wonder what's going to happen. Here are some of the usual steps.

Before the operation, you won't be able to eat or drink, and you'll need to put on a hospital gown.

An hour before the operation, you might have to take some medicine. It will make you sleepy, and your mouth might feel dry.

You might have some cream put on your hand so the needle for the anesthetic won't hurt.

Someone will come to get you when the doctor is ready to start. The anesthetic will make you sleep, so you won't feel a thing. If you want your parent to stay with you, ask about it as soon as you get to the hospital.

When you first wake up, you'll be in the recovery room. Then you'll be wheeled back to the ward on a flat, rolling cart called a gurney. You might sleep for a long time. Then, a nurse will bring something for you to drink.

Helping Yourself in the Hospital

When you have to go to the hospital, try to think of some ways to make yourself feel more comfortable. Here are some things you can do to help yourself get settled when you get to the ward:

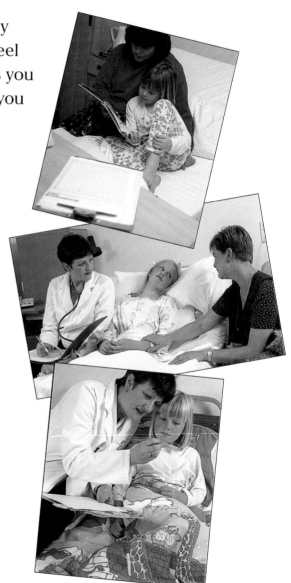

■ As soon as you can, learn your way around. Ask where the bathroom is. Find out when meals are served. See if there is a playroom. If there is, find out when you can visit it.

■ If you're going to have an operation, find out as much as you can about it. Ask a nurse to explain, step by step, what is going to happen.

■ Remember, all of the people around you want to help you get better. Help them to help you by telling them how you feel. Don't keep any worries or fears to yourself. If you will be in the hospital a long time, you can help yourself in other ways, too.

Keep yourself as busy as you can. Ask your family to bring in different things for you to do. Trade toys, games, and videos with other children on the ward. Try to learn how to do something new, such as braiding your hair, playing chess, or painting by numbers.

Use what you find out about hospital life to help someone else. Talk to new children on the ward and tell them what goes on there. You can help them feel more confident. Ask a nurse if there are any other ways you can help new patients get settled.

Keep in contact with friends at home and at school. Write them letters. Ask your parent or a nurse to help you record a tape to send them.

Like Jake, keep a hospital diary. Write notes about what happens each day during your stay. Then, when you get back home, you'll have a complete story about your time in the hospital to look back on.

Alex's Birthday

Alex sat straight up in bed and threw down the comic book he'd been reading. He wiggled his toes under the blanket and sighed. A nurse walked by and smiled at him, but Alex didn't smile back. He looked toward the door at the end of the children's ward. He could see his dad coming back with drinks from the vending machine. Alex closed his eyes and turned his face away.

"I got some Coke for you, Alex," his dad said. "I got some hot chocolate for myself. The coffee here is awful!"

Alex didn't say anything. He felt angry with his dad. He felt angry with everyone. In two days, it would be Alex's birthday. He would be eight years old — and he was in the hospital!

The next morning, Alex was awakened by someone whistling.
A nurse was checking the chart at the end of Alex's bed.

"Hi, I'm Harry!" said the nurse. "Your dad's getting some breakfast in the cafeteria."

Alex scowled.

"Wow," said Harry, "you're a grouch! Is that leg hurting you?"

"No," Alex snapped.

"Your operation's all set for this afternoon," said Harry. "I'll come to get you ready. If you have any questions, I'm your man. I'll tell you exactly what's going on. OK?"

Harry grinned, and Alex gave him a wobbly smile.

Harry looked into Alex's face, then back at the chart.

"Hey!" Harry said at last. "You're the Birthday Boy, aren't you? And you're stuck here for the big day. Right?"

"That's right," Alex said crossly.

"What kind of party were you planning?" asked Harry. "A picnic? Swimming?"

"The gym," Alex said quietly, "with pizzas afterward."

"Mmm," replied Harry, shaking his head. "There's no way you're doing any bouncing tomorrow, not with that leg."

"I know that!" snapped Alex. He thumped the mattress hard. "I'm trapped in this stupid bed!"

"Hey!" Harry said gently. "Life doesn't stop just because you're in the hospital, you know. A birthday's a birthday! Right?"

Alex shrugged. "What do you mean?" he asked.

"Wait and see!" grinned Harry.

That afternoon, Harry came back again. He got Alex ready for the operation on his leg. Harry explained everything that would happen. Soon, Alex was on a gurney, rolling toward the operating room. His dad squeezed Alex's hand as they moved down the hallway. All the while, Alex could hear Harry's friendly whistling in the background. It made things seem easier, somehow.

Later, Alex remembered someone calling his name. When he finally woke up, he was back in his bed. It was nighttime. His dad was asleep in a chair next to him.

Alex drifted back to sleep.

Alex spent the next morning opening birthday cards and presents with his dad. Then his mom came — with two computer games, a baseball glove, and a chess set made for traveling.

Alex heard Harry coming before he even saw him. Harry was whistling the tune "Happy Birthday to You!" And he was pushing a gurney piled high with boxes of pizza. A big red balloon was tied to the top of the stack.

"Party time, everyone!" called Harry.

He pulled up some more chairs, and children from beds all along the ward came to join in. Then a birthday cake arrived. It was big enough for them all to share. Harry turned off the lights, and everyone sang.

After Alex blew out the candles, he looked over at Harry and smiled. Harry winked.

"What did I tell you?" he asked.

"A birthday's a birthday — wherever you are!" laughed Alex.

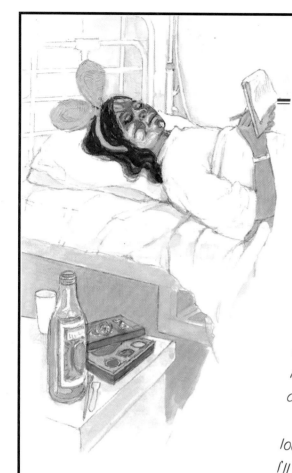

Dear Auntie Jan,

Thanks for coming and bringing me the face paints. We had fun with them.

I did what you said and told Mr. Green the teacher here about Sammie and Kim. We came up with the idea of making a tape for everyone at school. So I told them all about my operation and what it's like being in the hospital. Then I got a card from the whole class, and Sammie and Kim and some of the others came to visit me. Mrs. Barlow came, too. They said they're making a tape for me.

I'll be back in school next semester. I'm looking forward to it, but I'll miss everyone here. I'll need to come back, though, after six weeks, to be checked. Louise, the play leader here, says I can come in anytime to help out in the playroom.

Lots of Love,
Anna

Dear Anna,

Thank you for your letter and the crazy drawing of yourself! It's great. I put it on my bulletin board. It must be hard to draw when you're flat on your back.

I'm glad things have worked out so well for you and that you're looking forward to going back to school. After six weeks, you'll probably be really looking forward to going back to the hospital for your checkup. I imagine you'll find it a little strange to be an "outpatient" at the hospital, instead of staying there.

I'm sure your mom and dad will be happy to have you home. Give them my love.

Lots of love,
Auntie Jan

More Books to Read

- *The Doctor & You.*
  Diane Swanson
  (Annick Press)

- *Good-Bye Tonsils!*
  Juliana Lee Hatkoff and Craig Hatkoff
  (Viking Children's Books)

- *The Hospital Book.*
  James Howe
  (William Morrow & Co.)

- *Let's Talk About Going to the Hospital.*
  Marianne Johnston
  (Powerkids Press)

Web Sites

- Ever Been to a Hospital?
  www.faculty.fairfield.edu/fleitas/hospital.html

- Going to the Hospital.
  kidshealth.org/kid/feel_better/places/hospital.html